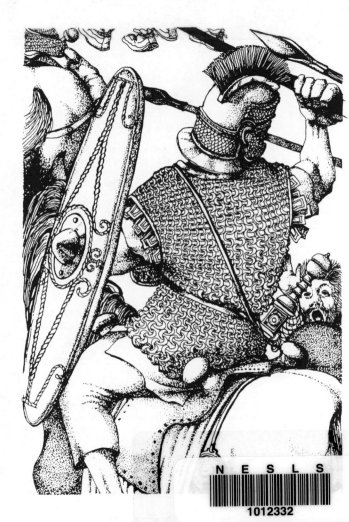

SCOTLAND IN ROMAN TIMES

Antony Kamm

Illustrated by Jennifer Campbell

SCOTTISH CHILDREN'S PRESS

First published 1998
Scottish Children's Press
Unit 14, Leith Walk Business Centre,
130 Leith Walk, Edinburgh, EH6 5DT
Tel: 0131 555 5950 • Fax: 0131 555 5018
e-mail: scp@sol.co.uk

Scottish Children's Press is an imprint of Scottish Cultural Press

British Library Cataloguing in Publication Data
A catalogue record for this book is available from the British Library

ISBN: 1 899827 14 5

The publisher acknowledges subsidy from the Scottish Arts Council
towards the publication of this book

*The distance slabs illustrated on pages 44 and 45, and the coins on
page 46, with many others of the Roman period, can be seen at the
Hunterian Museum, University of Glasgow*

Other books of interest from Scottish Children's Press
and Scottish Cultural Press

Antony Kamm: *Wallace, Bruce, and the War of Independence*,
illustrated by Jennifer Campbell;
1 899827 15 3

A D Cameron: *Discover Scotland's History*
1 898218 76 5

To receive complete, up-to-date catalogues
please contact the publisher

Printed and bound in Great Britain by
Cromwell Press Ltd, Trowbridge, Wiltshire

Contents

THE FIRST PEOPLES IN SCOTLAND

The first people came to Scotland about nine thousand years ago. They were hunters, who knew how to build rough boats in which to carry themselves and their belongings. They made tools out of stone, and spearheads, arrow heads, and fish hooks out of bone or antler. They wore clothing of skins and furs. Their food was fish from the sea, shellfish collected on the shores, and the meat of wild boar and red deer.

The first farmers arrived about seven thousand years ago. They brought their animals with them – cattle, sheep, and pigs. They grew wheat and other crops, and made pots of clay. Their homes were of wood or stone. They buried their dead in elaborate stone tombs dug into the ground.

In time they learned, possibly from craftsmen from the mainland of Europe, how to make things from copper and gold, which they could dig from the ground. They became traders, exchanging what they made for things they needed which came from other parts of Britain and from northern Europe. In particular they got tin from Cornwall in the south-west tip of Britain. They mixed the tin with copper to make weapons, tools, and ornaments of bronze. They also made gold armlets and neck rings, and necklaces of jet or amber beads.

About 2300 years ago a new people, the Celts, began to come to Britain from Europe.

The Coming of the Celts

The Celts had skills in farming and house-building which they had learned originally from people who came from Egypt and the Bible lands of the Middle East. They were a warlike race, whose iron weapons were stronger and sharper than any that had been known before. Gradually the Celts spread over the whole of Britain. They were not a united people. They were a collection of tribes who spent much of their time fighting each other for land, or in family feuds. About 2100 years ago (that is in about 100 BC) some Celtic tribes settled in Scotland.

TIME CHART OF EARLY SCOTLAND

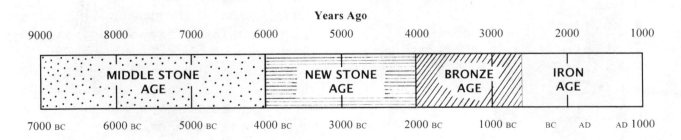

BC means 'Before Christ'. AD is Latin, *Anno Domini,* which means 'In the Year of the Lord'.

THE CELTS IN SCOTLAND

The chief of a Celtic tribe could be a man or a woman. After the chief came the nobles and the wise men. There were three kinds of wise men. The druids (or priests) were believed to be able to perform magic. The seers were supposed to be able to see into the future. The bards sang songs and tales of magic and of brave deeds. Below them were the farmers, craftsmen, and metal-workers, who had their own pieces of land. Then came the slaves, who had nothing.

One Roman writer mentions the 'amazing clothes' of the Celts. Their shirts and tunics were brightly-coloured. Men wore trousers. Their moustaches were often so long that it was difficult to eat or drink through them. Both men and women wore ornamental rings of gold or bronze round their necks and arms.

Another Roman writer describes the Celts who lived in Scotland as having red hair and big limbs. They made clothes from wool, leather, and animal skins. In the cold northern climate, a thick woollen cloak, possibly woven in a check pattern, would have been essential.

Celtic feasts were held in a big round house or in the open air. The guests sat on the ground around the central hearth, in order of their importance. Behind each warrior stood his armour-bearer. Food, which included bread, was served on low tables. Roast or boiled pork was a favourite dish. The best piece of meat was known as the Champion's Portion, and went to the bravest man. The drink was usually beer. Celts also ate beef, mutton, and fish, which was often salted and baked.

Celts were noisy and fierce in war. They cheered and yelled and blew trumpets to frighten their opponents. They fought in chariots, as well as on foot. Some went into battle naked, which they believed gave them magical protection, or painted patterns on their bodies. A warrior would return with the heads of defeated enemies hanging from his chariot rail.

Celts in Scotland lived in fortified homes or in hilltop villages surrounded by walls of heavy stones. Apart from the danger from unfriendly tribes, bears and wolves roamed wild in Scotland then.

Forests were cleared for wood to build homes, and to provide spaces for cattle and sheep to graze, and for wheat and barley to be grown. Pigs foraged for food wherever they could find it. Meat was boiled or cooked in animal fat. Fat was also used to fuel lamps and to make soap. Craftsmen, particularly in south-west Scotland around Dumfries, worked in gold, as well as in iron and bronze.

There were several kinds of homes specially built against attackers. A *dun* was a round or oval fort. The living space was often in compartments in the main wall. A *crannog* was a round wood and thatched house built on an artificial island in a loch. It was joined to the land by a narrow wooden pathway hidden under the surface of the water. People in Scotland went on living in crannogs until about AD 1450.

The most extraordinary remains of Celtic Scotland are the *brochs,* made of roughly-shaped stones without any mortar or cement to hold them together. Brochs were first built in about 100 BC and continued to be lived in for six hundred years. They were about 15 metres across and as high as a four-storey block of modern flats. There were no openings on the outside except for one tiny entrance into a tunnel. People lived inside the thick walls in rooms connected by a winding stone staircase.

Brochs are known only in Scotland. Since most of those built at this time are on the north and east coasts, they would seem to have been intended as defences against raiders coming by ship over the North Sea. Whatever it was that the broch people feared, when the Roman invasion of Scotland came, it was on foot, and from the south.

WHO WERE THE ROMANS?

According to the Romans themselves, the city of Rome was founded on 21 April 753 BC by Romulus, who became its first king. Another story traces the beginnings of Rome back to about 1200 BC, with the arrival of the Trojan hero Aeneas, who was the son of a human father and of the goddess Venus.

The Romans got rid of being ruled by kings in 510 BC. For almost five hundred years after that the government was in the hands of elected officials, advised by assemblies. The most important of these assemblies was the senate. It consisted of about three hundred members, most of whom had themselves served as government officials.

The Romans needed to protect themselves against people that might attack them. The Celts were particularly troublesome. In 390 BC some of them even occupied Rome for a time, before being bribed with gold to go home. They did not go far. By 340 BC Celts had settled throughout the northern part of what is now Italy.

The Romans also needed land to support their growing population. They got it by conquering the peoples who lived in it. By 170 BC they had conquered the whole of Italy, including the Celtic lands in the north.

Julius Caesar, who was born in 102 BC, tried to rule the Romans on his own by legal means. He was murdered in 44 BC by a group of discontented officials, former soldiers, and members of the senate. He was succeeded by his adopted son and heir, Augustus, who is regarded as the first Roman emperor.

The language of the Romans was Latin. Copies of books, especially of history and poetry, were written out by slaves on rolls of paper made from the papyrus reed, and sold in bookshops.

Ordinary wear for both men and women, and also for slaves, was a belted tunic with short sleeves. The male tunic reached to the knees: women and girls wore theirs longer. In winter you might wear two tunics, one on top of the other. Augustus, who suffered badly from the cold, sometimes used to wear four.

Formal wear for freeborn men, and also for boys, was the *toga*. This was an outer garment like an enormous woollen blanket, made in the form of part of a circle, with one straight side and

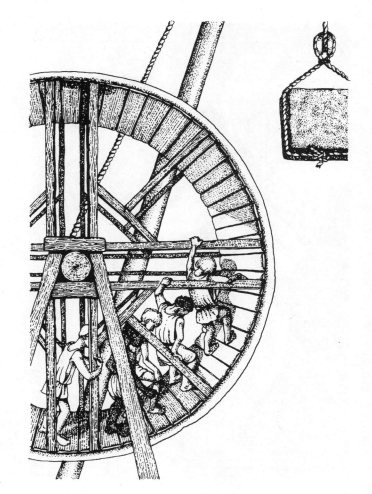

one curved side. It was about five metres long, and two metres deep at its widest point. It was draped round and over the body, leaving one arm free. Out of doors women wore a similar garment, the *palla,* which was a rectangle in shape. Men who were standing for election to public office whitened their *toga* with chalk. They were known as *candidati,* which means 'clothed in glittering white'; from this comes our word 'candidate'.

Most of the Roman work force were slaves, who did all the heavy labour and were also the household servants. Slaves worked on the farms, in the mines, and in the potteries. They were the

The Romans had many gods and goddesses. They also believed that there were spirits everywhere in nature, and even in household objects. By praying or making a sacrifice (which could be food or drink), the Romans hoped to get a favour in return. They also believed in omens. They watched birds flying or examined the insides of sacrificed animals, to see what the future might bring. A flash of lightning usually meant that something bad was about to happen.

state's building workers and also its clerks and administrators. Slaves could buy their freedom or obtain it by arrangement with their masters. Doctors (female as well as male), dentists, surgeons, teachers, architects, and farm managers were often freed slaves.

Freeborn women were able to get some education, but few of them had jobs outside the home. Freeborn men usually followed the trades or crafts of their fathers. When opportunities for small farmers began to grow less in about 200 BC, many men looked to the army to provide their living.

Though the Romans went to theatres to see plays acted on the stage, their two favourite entertainments were chariot races and the games. At the games trained gladiators, who were slaves, fought each other to the death, or hunted and killed (or were killed by) wild animals. Animals were made to fight each other – lions against tigers, elephants against bulls, even bears against seals.

THE ROMAN ARMY

The Roman army was the most efficient fighting force the world has ever known. Its strength was in its organisation and in the training of its ordinary foot-soldiers, the legionaries.

Up to the time of Julius Caesar, legionaries were Roman citizens, who volunteered for at least six years. Later, men served in the army for 25 years. Until about AD 200 they were not allowed to marry during their term of service.

On the march, a legionary wore his helmet, his armour, and his sword, and carried his shield and two javelins (of different weights). He also carried, on a forked pole, his spare clothes and personal belongings, three days' rations of food and drink, and cooking equipment: and for making camp, at the end of each day's march, a sharp digging tool, a saw, a sickle for cutting grass and scrub, a basket with which to shift earth, and a piece of rope for handling bits of turf.

Augustus established a permanent army of 28 legions. Each legion, which consisted of about six thousand men, was a self-contained army in itself. In addition to the legionaries and their officers, there were men who performed particular tasks.

The *aquilifer* carried the legion's standard. With him was the *imaginifer,* who carried a standard bearing medallions and portraits of the emperor and past emperors. A bugler blew the *cornu,* a circular horn, in battle to show where the legion's standard was. Another wind instrument, the *tuba,* a long trumpet, sounded the advance and retreat in battle, and in camp indicated that it was time for the sentries to change.

The legion's specialists and craftsmen were known as *immunes* (excused normal duties). They included surveyors, master builders, medical orderlies, gunners, armourers, carpenters, hunters (to kill animals for food), engineers, and clerks. A legion had several catapults, able to fire large rocks. Each century also had the use of a mechanical arrow-shooter.

A legion was often supported by auxiliary troops, comprising cavalry and additional infantry, made up of inhabitants of the empire who were not Roman citizens. They were commanded originally by their own chiefs, but later by Roman officers.

THE ROMAN LEGION

Centurion

Legatus
Legate
Commander of a legion, a post held for about three years

Tribunus Laticlavius
Senior Tribune
Young man of noble birth

Praefectus Castrorum
Camp Prefect
Senior professional soldier in the legion: in charge of the camp
and its equipment (including artillery and medical services), and
of training

Tribuni
Junior tribunes (5)
Advisers and assistants to the legate

A LEGION CONSISTED OF 10 COHORTS. THE FIRST COHORT
CONTAINED 5 CENTURIES, EACH OF 160 MEN:
THE OTHER 9 CONTAINED 6 CENTURIES OF 80 MEN

Centurion
Commander of a century. The senior centurion in the legion
was called the Centurio Primi Pili and
commanded the first century of the first cohort

Signifer
Carried the century's standard and looked after its savings bank

Optio
Second-in-command of a century in battle

Tesserarius
In charge of sentries and work parties

Custos Armorum
In charge of weapons and equipment

Legionaries
Eight men shared a tent, which on the march was
rolled up and carried by a mule or pony.

Signifer

THE ROMAN EMPIRE

The Romans needed their army to protect themselves against peoples from outside. The army had to be paid. Its officers and men wanted the spoils and loot which were the rewards of a conquering army. Roman life depended largely on slave labour. A ready supply of slaves came from peoples whom the Romans defeated in war.

So the Roman empire expanded, far beyond Italy and all round the coast of the Mediterranean Sea. All but a part of the Celtic land of Spain became Roman in 197 BC: two tribes in the north held out until 19 BC. The Celts in their homeland of Gaul were finally crushed by Julius Caesar in 50 BC after a ruthless eight-year campaign. In 55 BC and again in 54 BC he had crossed over to Britain, but after fighting a few battles and taking some hostages, he decided to leave the Celts there to look after themselves.

The empire provided money in the form of taxes, and also many of the things which the Romans needed to keep their rich in luxury and their poorer citizens in food.

The most famous chief in Gaul was Vercingetorix, whose skill as a general was for a time equal to Caesar's. He was finally besieged in Alesia. The town was starved into surrender, and Vercingetorix gave himself up. After being kept in prison in Rome, he was made to march in chains in one of the triumphal processions in 46 BC with which Caesar also celebrated his victories in Africa and Asia over his political opponents. When the procession was over, Vercingetorix was put to death.

Many people in the city of Rome itself were supplied with free corn, which they made into bread or porridge. The corn came mainly from north Africa, Egypt, and Sicily, by sea to the port of Rome at Ostia. The Celtic lands of Europe provided metals – copper, tin, iron, lead, brass, bronze, silver, and gold – as well as timber, glass, pottery, cloth, hides from which to make leather, wine, and olive oil for cooking.

Julius Caesar dealt cruelly with the people of Gaul. Whole towns were sold off to slave dealers.

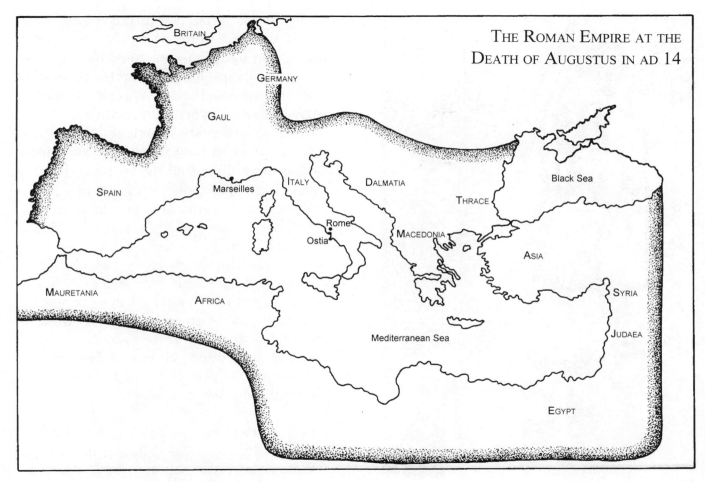

THE ROMAN EMPIRE AT THE
DEATH OF AUGUSTUS IN AD 14

BRITAIN

GERMANY

GAUL

SPAIN

Marseilles

ITALY

DALMATIA

Black Sea

THRACE

Rome

MACEDONIA

ASIA

Ostia

MAURETANIA

AFRICA

SYRIA

JUDAEA

Mediterranean Sea

EGYPT

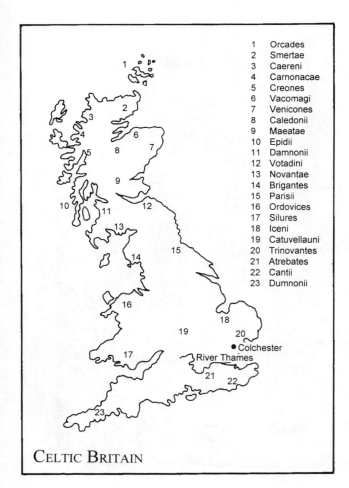

1	Orcades
2	Smertae
3	Caereni
4	Carnonacae
5	Creones
6	Vacomagi
7	Venicones
8	Caledonii
9	Maeatae
10	Epidii
11	Damnonii
12	Votadini
13	Novantae
14	Brigantes
15	Parisii
16	Ordovices
17	Silures
18	Iceni
19	Catuvellauni
20	Trinovantes
21	Atrebates
22	Cantii
23	Dumnonii

CELTIC BRITAIN

THE INVASION OF BRITAIN

Augustus left instructions that the Roman empire was now big enough, and that his successors should not try to enlarge it. When Claudius became emperor in AD 41, he decided that something should be done about Britain.

Claudius needed personal military glory if he was to gain the confidence of his army. He also needed money. The Celts in Britain had become rich through trade, particularly in gold, silver, and other metals. They would be easy to defeat, because they were not united.

In AD 43 Claudius sent his general, Aulus Plautius, to Britain with four legions. Plautius made some progress, but the death of one of the tribal chiefs, so far from causing the tribes to panic, united them in a determination to avenge his killing. What happened next is described by Dio Cassius, who lived at the end of the second century AD and wrote in Greek:

Plautius settled his troops in and sent for Claudius. Those were his orders if he met any resistance, and great preparations had already been made, including the mobilisation of a team of battle elephants. Claudius went by river to Ostia, and then sailed along the coast to Marseilles. From there, travelling overland and by river, he reached the sea and crossed to Britain, where he met up with his troops, who were encamped by the river Thames. Taking command, he crossed the river, engaged the barbarians,* who had rallied together at his approach, defeated them, and took Colchester. Then he put down many other tribes, defeating them or accepting their surrender.

Only a part of Britain had been conquered. Some of the tribes did not like Roman rule, and rebelled against it. Other tribes made peace with the Romans.

Claudius was poisoned by his wife in AD 54. There were four emperors between him and Vespasian, who in AD 77 appointed Gnaeus Julius Agricola to complete the conquest of Britain.

* The Romans called everyone a 'barbarian' who lived outside the Roman empire.

It is said that among those who submitted to Roman rule after Claudius's victory were the Orcades, whose leaders came all the way from Orkney to the south of Britain to do so.

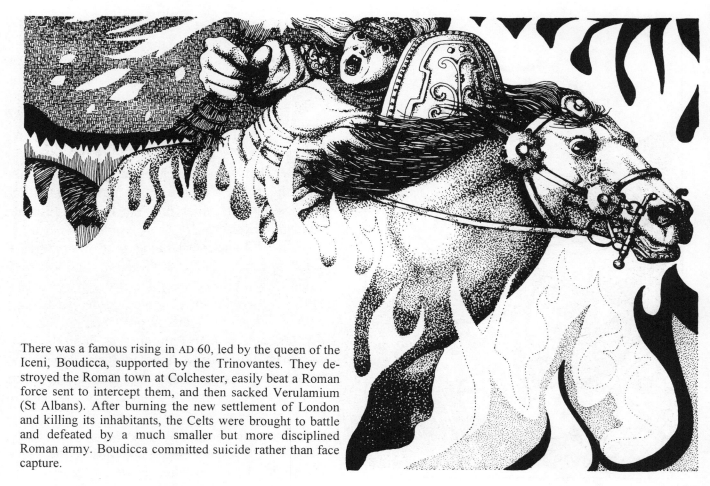

There was a famous rising in AD 60, led by the queen of the Iceni, Boudicca, supported by the Trinovantes. They destroyed the Roman town at Colchester, easily beat a Roman force sent to intercept them, and then sacked Verulamium (St Albans). After burning the new settlement of London and killing its inhabitants, the Celts were brought to battle and defeated by a much smaller but more disciplined Roman army. Boudicca committed suicide rather than face capture.

AGRICOLA'S CAMPAIGNS IN
SCOTLAND AD 79–83

AGRICOLA, GOVERNOR OF BRITAIN

We know about Agricola because Tacitus (who was his son-in-law) wrote a biography of him. Agricola's first task was to put down a rebellion by the Ordovices in north Wales. Then in AD 79 he advanced into Scotland by an eastern route. He met more resistance, Tacitus tells us, from the weather than from the tribes in his way. As they went, his soldiers built forts, to make sure that the regions through which they passed would remain Roman territory.

In AD 80 and 81 Agricola's army explored a western route, and established a line of forts along the valleys between the firths of Clyde and Forth. Agricola also sent ships up the west coast, perhaps as far as Cape Wrath, before deciding that his route to the north must be along the eastern coast. There were too many mountains and lochs on the western side.

In AD 82 he again advanced by the eastern route. His ships went ahead, landing raiding parties of marines whose sudden attacks terrified the Celts along the coast. The Caledonians, the Celtic tribe in northern Scotland, showed no fear.

The Roman army built roads wherever it could, to ensure that there were communications with the city of Rome, and also that troops could more easily be moved around the country. There were finally about 800 kilometres (500 miles) of Roman roads in Scotland, with a milestone, only one of which has so far been found, at every Roman mile. Roman roads followed a direct line wherever possible. Those in Scotland were about 6 m wide. A layer of crushed rock and pebbles was spread on top of a bed of stones. The surface was slightly curved to allow water to drain off at each side.

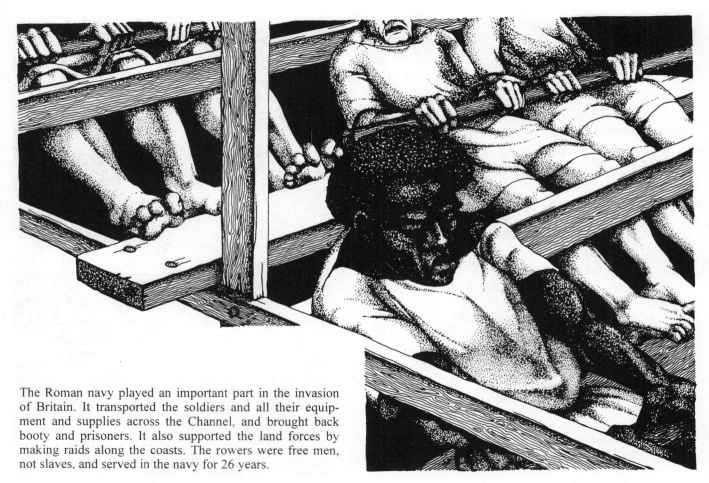

The Roman navy played an important part in the invasion of Britain. It transported the soldiers and all their equipment and supplies across the Channel, and brought back booty and prisoners. It also supported the land forces by making raids along the coasts. The rowers were free men, not slaves, and served in the navy for 26 years.

The Caledonians attacked the Roman columns so often and so fiercely that some of Agricola's officers advised him to retreat. This he refused to do. The Caledonians even made a night assault on the Ninth Legion as it slept. They would have overrun the camp if Agricola had not suddenly appeared with reinforcements,

By AD 83 both sides were keen for a real battle. The Caledonians had persuaded other Celtic tribes to join them and make a united force. Agricola's term of office as governor of Britain was ending, and he would shortly be recalled to Rome.

Later, the Ninth Legion disappears from the records. We know that it was still stationed at York in AD 108, after which it was transferred to Germany. Scholars think that it may have been destroyed in the fighting in Palestine in AD 132 or lost in the Asian province of Cappadocia in AD 161.

THE BATTLE OF MONS GRAUPIUS

We do not know exactly where the great battle took place. Tacitus simply calls it Mons Graupius* (the Graupian mountain). Thirty thousand Celts were waiting. They chose as their leader Calgacus, which means 'swordsman'.

Agricola marched his men there. They had left all their baggage at their base, and so had only their weapons to carry. He put his auxiliaries, who included British Celts as well as Celts from Gaul, into the front line, with the infantry in the middle and the cavalry on each side. The rest of his cavalry was lined up behind them. The Roman legions were in the rear; in the end they were not needed.

* Historians believe that Mons Graupius may have been Mount Bennachie, near Aberdeen. In an edition of Tacitus's biography of Agricola printed in about AD 1470, Graupius was wrongly spelled as Grampius. The mistake is still with us today: in Grampian Television, Grampian Mountains, and other uses of the word.

Here is part of Tacitus's description of the battle:

First, both sides stood and hurled their spears at each other. The enemy showed great skill in fending them off with their light shields and with the blades of their huge swords. Then Agricola ordered six cohorts of auxiliaries to engage them.

The enemy were not used to hand-to-hand fighting and their swords, which had no points, were useless at such close range. Our auxiliaries pushed them furiously up the slope.

Meanwhile, our cavalry, having put the enemy chariots to flight, joined up with our infantry. The force of the charge was terrific, but our infantry was finding the slope a problem, while empty chariots and frantic riderless horses added to the confusion.

So far, the rest of the enemy forces had stayed at the top of the hill. They had thought they would win easily, for they outnumbered us by far. They now started to descend, to try and get round behind our front line. Agricola was expecting this move.

He launched at them the four wings of cavalry

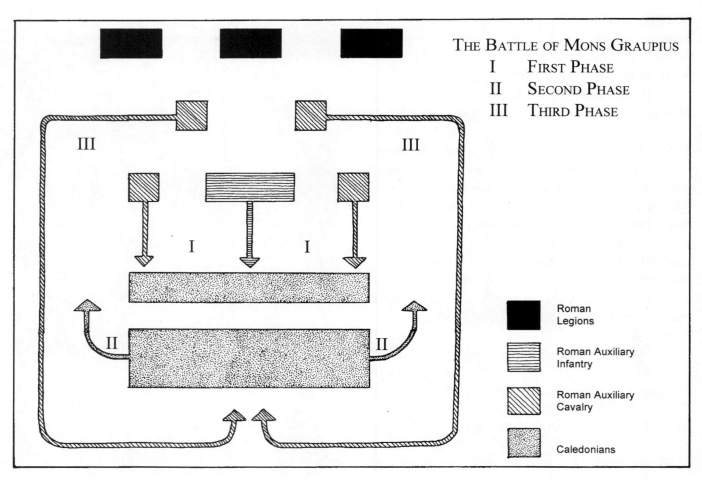

THE BATTLE OF MONS GRAUPIUS
I   FIRST PHASE
II   SECOND PHASE
III THIRD PHASE

Roman Legions

Roman Auxiliary Infantry

Roman Auxiliary Cavalry

Caledonians

which he had kept in reserve. In a moment, the enemy's advance turned into a retreat. And the well-disciplined Roman cavalry which was already in the fighting extricated itself, formed up again, wheeled round behind the enemy and took them in the rear.

The field of battle presented a ghastly sight. The surviving Caledonians fled into the wooded countryside, where they were hunted down by the Roman cavalry and light infantry. Some of the Caledonian wounded were carried away by their wailing womanfolk. After the Romans had spent the night celebrating their victory, Agricola sent out scouts to make sure that the survivors had not got together again. The hills and woods were silent. There was no one to be seen: only smoking houses which the Caledonians had burned after moving out of them.

Agricola led his victorious army back to its permanent camps for the winter. He sent his ships to explore the north coast of Scotland. They sailed along its whole length to Cape Wrath, where they turned back, having proved that Britain was an island.

Satisfied now that he had done a good job, Agricola wrote a report to his emperor in Rome in which he modestly described his various achievements.

Roman Fortifications in Scotland

In many parts of Scotland there are signs of Roman marching camps. Some are about 25 km apart, which was a normal day's march. At the end of each day's march, the legionaries dug a ditch and built a fence of wooden stakes behind it, using the tools and stakes which they carried with them. Inside the fence they put up leather tents for their officers and for themselves, with streets and open spaces between, like a miniature town.

A fort was a permanent base, usually for auxiliaries. In Scotland, the buildings inside the fort had timber frames supporting wattled walls covered with clay. (Wattled means made of wooden poles or sticks interwoven crosswise with twigs.) The roofs were of timber or thatch. The buildings included a headquarters block, a house for the commander, and a bath-house. The soldiers lived, slept, and cooked for themselves in barrack blocks.

Cleanliness was a part of Roman life, and all permanent army bases had a bath-house, which in some cases contained a pool big enough to swim in. Bath-houses in Scotland were quite small, and consisted of a series of stone-built rooms, away from the main buildings because of the risk of fire from the furnaces. After undressing, you went through successively hotter rooms, scraped off the sweat and dirt, and then had a cold plunge to close the pores. The rooms were centrally-heated by hot air blown under the floor and up pipes behind the walls.

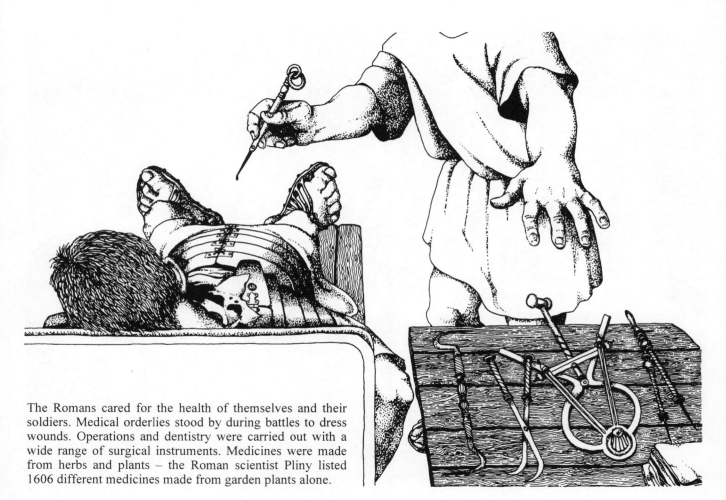

The Romans cared for the health of themselves and their soldiers. Medical orderlies stood by during battles to dress wounds. Operations and dentistry were carried out with a wide range of surgical instruments. Medicines were made from herbs and plants – the Roman scientist Pliny listed 1606 different medicines made from garden plants alone.

There are traces in southern Scotland of many Roman forts which were built and occupied at about the time when Agricola began his Scottish campaigns. Shortly after he was recalled to Rome, work began on a huge fortress at Inchtuthil, Perthshire, to be the permanent base for an entire legion. It covered an area of 21.7 hectares. One of its features was a hospital (91 m long and 59 m wide), with sixty wards, each to contain five beds.

Before it could be finished, the fortress was carefully destroyed by its builders, so that nothing could be used by the native Celts. Some things which the Romans could not take with them, like pottery and glass, they smashed. Other things, including one million brand-new nails, they buried. The legion for which the fortress was being built was needed to protect Rome from enemies nearer home.

HADRIAN'S WALL

The Romans believed in helping the peoples of the Roman empire. In the southern parts of Britain, Agricola assisted the Celtic population to think and become more like Romans: to live in well-designed towns and houses, to enjoy Roman food and entertainment, and to believe in Roman as well as Celtic gods. This did not happen in Scotland, where military roads and fortifications were the only reminders that the Romans had been there.

Gradually the Roman army abandoned Scotland and retreated to a line between Corbridge and Carlisle known as the Stanegate, a road along which were a number of forts and watch-towers. The emperor Hadrian, on a visit to Britain in AD 122, recognised that something stronger was required if the northern Celts were to be prevented actually from invading Roman Britain.

The Romans were marvellous builders and engineers. They knew about cranes and pulleys, mortar and concrete, brick-making and brick-laying, and about water pressure. They made

Army buildings in Scotland were made of shaped stones or of wood. Roman brick walls were not entirely brick. Triangular bricks were used, with an inner core of concrete.

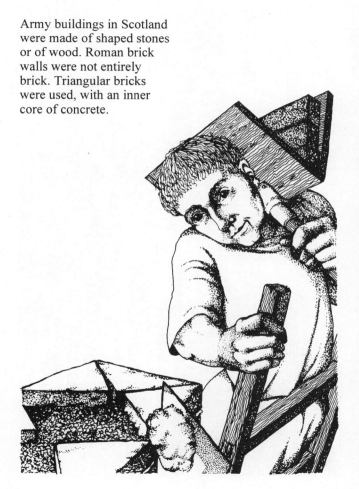

Part of an aqueduct in Segovia, Spain, 29 m high and still in working order

strong, straight roads. Above all, they knew how to use the arch to support heavy weights: to build stone bridges to carry roads across rivers, and aqueducts to carry water courses overhead and across valleys. They had accurate instruments to measure distances, height, and length. A Roman foot *(pes)* and the longer unit, a pace *(passus)*, were precise measurements.

> 1 Roman foot = $11^5/_8$ inches = 29.59 cm
> 5 Roman feet = 1 pace = 4 ft $10^1/_4$ inches = 1.48 m
> 1000 paces *(mille passus)* = 1 Roman mile = 1618 yards = 1.48 km

Hadrian's Wall was an enormous fortified barrier of stone and turf, about 5 m high and between 3 m and 1.8 m wide, with battlements on top. It ran for 117 km (73 miles) from coast to coast. It had additional lines of defence, consisting of continuous lines of ditches and earth mounds. There were seventeen forts along its length, and a tower at every Roman mile. Between each tower and the next were two fortified turrets.

ROMAN NUMBERS

All Roman numbers were written by using one or more of the letters I, V, X, L, C, D, M. Nought (0) was not used. Sums were done on one's fingers or by moving beads on a counting frame.

I	1	XII	12	L	50
II	2	XIII	13	C	100
III	3	XIV (one less than 15)	14	D	500
IIII or IV (one less than 5)	4	XV	15	M	1000
V	5	XVI (one more than 15)	16		
VI (one more than 5)	6	XVII	17	Years are sometimes written in	
VII	7	XVIII	18	Roman numbers:	
VIII	8	XIX (one less than 20)	19	1998	MCMXCVIII
IX (one less than 10)	9	XX	20	1999	MCMXCIX
X	10	XXX	30	2000	MM
XI (one more than 10)	11	XL (ten less than 50)	40	2001	MMI

THE ROMAN CALENDAR

- The twelve months of the Roman calendar each contained three special days.
- The *calends* were always on the first of the month.
- The *ides* were on the 13th of January, February, April, June, August, September, November, and December, and on the 15th of March, May, July, and October.
- The *nones* were on the ninth day before the ides, including the day at each end of the period. So the nones of March were on 7 March.
- The Roman day was divided into twelve hours of equal length from sunrise to sunset (first hour, second hour, and so on), and the night likewise. So the length of the hour, and the time at which it began and ended, varied according to the season of the year.
- We say a.m. when we mean *ante meridiem,* Latin for 'before the middle of the day', and p.m., *post meridiem,* for 'after the middle of the day'. The Romans used sundials or water-clocks, or a combination of both, to tell the time.

THE ANTONINE WALL

Hadrian's successor as emperor, Antoninus, ordered his army to advance beyond Hadrian's Wall and to push hostile Celtic tribes farther north. When this had been done, a second wall was built in about AD 142, stretching for 60 km (37 miles) between the firths of Clyde and Forth.

The Antonine Wall was made of layers of turf on a base of sandstone rocks. There was a defensive ditch in front, and a military road ran all the way along its southern side. Forts, mainly manned by auxiliaries, were placed at regular intervals along its length. Further forts, with connecting roads, were built between the Antonine Wall and Hadrian's Wall. These were to ensure that the peace was kept between the two walls, and that there were reinforcements available if there should be trouble from the Celtic tribes beyond the Antonine Wall.

Men of the Second, Sixth, and Twentieth legions built the Antonine Wall and its forts. We know who built which part of the whole of the western half of the wall from the distance slabs which have been found. Each one names the legion responsible for a particular section, with its exact length, in paces or Roman feet.

The inscription says that this part of the wall was built by men of the Sixth Legion for the emperor Antoninus, a distance of 3240 (MMMCCXL) feet. The figures underneath are, from the left: Mars, the Roman god of war; two winged figures of Victory, each with her hair up; a female warrior representing bravery in war. Length 1.19 m: height 0.76 m: thickness 0.18 m.

FORTS ALONG THE ANTONINE WALL
showing existing sites

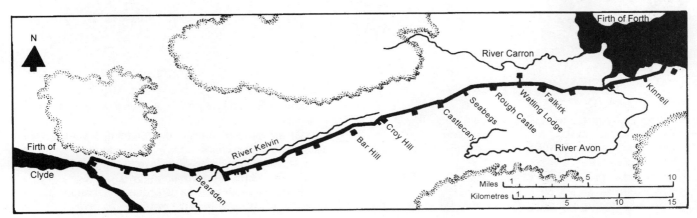

 (a)

 (b)

 (c)

 (d)

 (e)

 (f)

 (g)

ROMAN MONEY

All actual size

a) copper *quadrans:* the smallest Roman coin. It was the fee for entrance to the public baths in Rome.

b) brass *semis* with head of the emperor Domitian (worth two *quadrantes*).

c) copper *as* with head of Hadrian, the wall builder (worth two *semisses*).

d) brass *dupondius* with head of Caracalla (real name Antoninus), celebrating his victories in Britain (worth two *asses*).

e) brass *sestertius* with head of Antoninus, the wall builder (worth two *dupondii*).

f) silver *denarius* with head of Severus, celebrating his victories in Britain (worth four *sestertii*).

g) gold *aureus* with head of Claudius, celebrating his successful invasion of Britain (worth 25 *denarii*).

Roman soldiers guarding the Antonine Wall had a balanced diet. Corn was supplied by the army. Each group of men ground it for themselves into flour in a stone handmill to make bread, biscuits, porridge, and pasta dishes. They ate cheese, nuts, local vegetables, fruit, fish, and shellfish. Meat, when it was eaten, was beef, mutton, or (more usually) bacon. They drank raw wine or Celtic beer – many of the auxiliaries were themselves Celts. Examination of human deposits in the lavatory next to the Bearsden bath-house has shown that the soldiers there had eaten strawberries, raspberries, and figs, and bread flavoured with poppy seeds and coriander, and had taken various herbs for medicinal purposes.

The bath-house was not just for getting clean. In its heated rooms off-duty soldiers relaxed, chatted, drank their wine or beer, and played dice and board games, gambling on the results.

Instead of loo paper, Romans used balls of moss or sponge on sticks, which they washed in the channel of running water on the floor.

As well as the Celtic language, the Picts spoke a language used in Scotland before the Celts came there. They carved it into stone, in letters called ogham, an alphabet probably invented in Ireland in about AD 300. We can read the letters but we do not understand much of the language. There are Pictish carvings also of people, animals, birds, fish, household objects, and intricate curly designs.

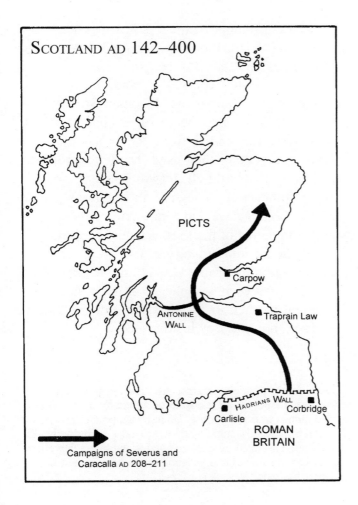

SCOTLAND AD 142–400

PICTS

Carpow

ANTONINE WALL

Traprain Law

HADRIANS WALL

Carlisle

Corbridge

ROMAN BRITAIN

Campaigns of Severus and Caracalla AD 208–211

THE KINGDOM OF THE PICTS

When the trouble did come from the Celtic tribes, it was almost too much for the Romans. They repaired the Antonine Wall and the damaged forts, and hung on – but not for long. In about AD 165, the Antonine Wall was abandoned by the Romans. By about AD 180, the northern frontier of Roman Britain was once again Hadrian's Wall.

Rumblings of revolt continued north of the wall. In AD 209 the emperor himself, Septimius Severus, led a massive invasion into Scotland against the Maeatae and the Caledonians. A temporary peace was made. The Romans began to build a new legionary fortress at Carpow. The next year there was another rebellion, which was put down by Caracalla, Severus's son. The Romans, however, had had enough, and Carpow was abandoned. It is probable that for the next hundred years trade continued between the friendlier Celtic tribes just to the north of Hadrian's Wall and the Roman soldiers still manning the forts in those parts. The Votadini, with their strong hillfort on Traprain Law, are said to have been especially favoured.

49

A new grouping of the Celtic tribes was now taking place. Together they became known as the Picts, meaning 'painted people'. They attacked Hadrian's Wall repeatedly, and even broke through the wall and invaded Roman Britain.

The Picts are first heard of in about AD 300. They were descended from the broch builders. Where they could, they used the stones from ruined brochs to build clusters of homes round the ancient broch wall. They are a mysterious people largely because we have no written records of them, only a list of their kings from about AD 555. It was the custom among the Picts that the kingship passed through the female line. A king could be succeeded by his brother, that is by the son of his royal mother, or by his sister's or his daughter's son, but never by his own son.

The Celts in Scotland did not use money, though Roman coins have been found in places occupied by them. Usually the Romans traded with the Celtic tribes near the walls for building materials, hay for their animals, fuel, foodstuffs, and beer. The local people received in exchange jewellery, glassware, or manufactured goods such as pots, bowls, and leather footwear.

Whithorn in Galloway was once known by the Latin name of *Candida Casa* (White House). It may have been a centre of trade in Roman times. St Ninian, a Celt of noble birth, probably from Cumbria, studied in Rome, from which he was sent as a bishop to preach to the southern Picts. He established at Whithorn the earliest known Christian church in Scotland. His actual dates are uncertain; we only know that he lived at some time between about AD 370 and 550.

THE FINAL ROMAN RETREAT

Celts from the Irish tribe of Dal Riata first came to Scotland as allies of the Picts. They were known as Scotti (or Scots), which probably means 'raiders' or 'pirates'. They joined the Picts in their raids on Roman Britain.

In AD 367 something extraordinary happened. The Picts and the Scots, and from Europe the Franks and the Saxons, got together to make attacks at the same time by land and by sea on the Roman defences in Britain and Gaul. The Roman secret police either did not know about the plan or had been bribed to say nothing.

The joint attacks were so sudden, and so successful, that both the army and the naval Roman commanders in Britain were killed. The raiders even penetrated the countryside round London.

While the Picts concentrated on the remaining forts round Hadrian's Wall and attacked the Wall itself, the Scots struck along the western coast and even penetrated into Wales.

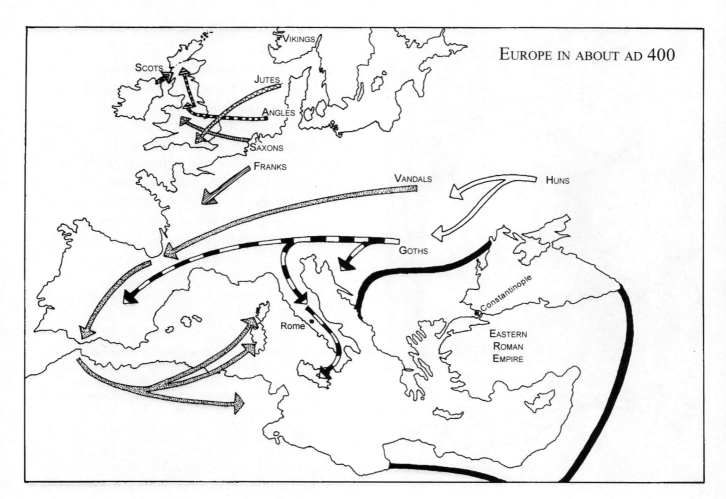

EUROPE IN ABOUT AD 400

SCOTS

VIKINGS

JUTES

ANGLES

SAXONS

FRANKS

VANDALS

HUNS

GOTHS

Constantinople

Rome

EASTERN ROMAN EMPIRE

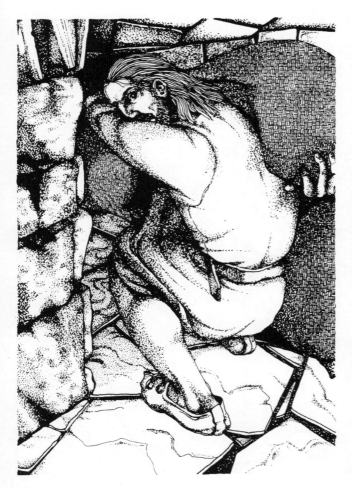

It took the Romans two years to restore order south of Hadrian's Wall. North of the Wall, the Picts, free from Roman control, carried on with their normal lives: farming, herding flocks, fishing, and waging tribal warfare.

Meanwhile the rest of the Roman empire was being attacked by hordes of Vandals and Goths, who had overrun central and western Europe and were now threatening Italy. In about AD 400 the Roman legions in Britain were rushed back to the final defence of the city of Rome itself.

Remains have been found in particular parts of Scotland of Pictish earth-houses, of which one at Crichton, Midlothian, was constructed in about AD 150 using stones from a Roman fort which had been abandoned or destroyed. Earth-houses were underground tunnels lined and roofed with stone slabs, often with a drain running under the floor-stones. The entrance was in a hut above the ground. It is thought that they were used for storing meat and grain. Similar tunnels have been discovered in Ireland under forts built by the Scots.

Which Celtic woman was Empress of Rome, worked for the Christian Church in Britain, and was the mother of kings? The answer is Elen Luyddog ('Elen of the Hosts'). She was the daughter of a Welsh chieftain. She married a Roman general from Spain, Magnus Maximus, who was serving in Britain. In AD 382 he defeated an army of Caledonians and Irish Celts. His own men, fed up with being so far from Rome, declared him Emperor of the Celtic lands of Britain, Gaul, and Spain. After defeating and killing the existing Emperor, Magnus ruled from Gaul, until in AD 388 he was himself captured and put to death. Elen, having become a Christian, returned to Britain with her children. Her work is remembered now in the word 'elen' in many Welsh place names. Her sons or their descendants ruled in south Wales, Kent, and the Isle of Man.

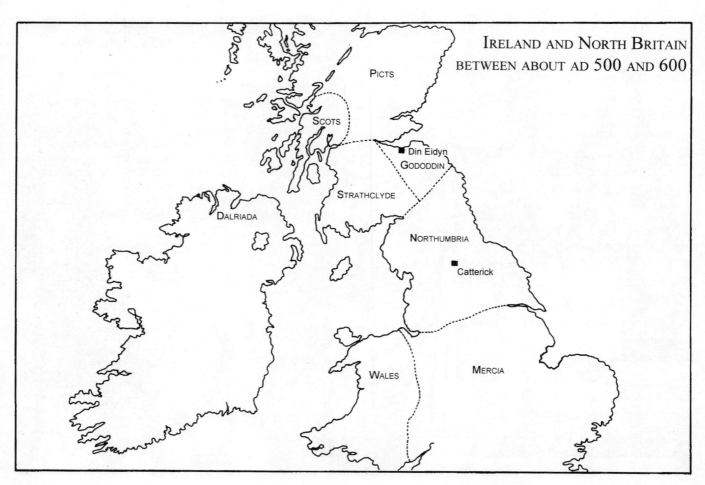

IRELAND AND NORTH BRITAIN
BETWEEN ABOUT AD 500 AND 600

PICTS

SCOTS

Din Eidyn
GODODDIN

STRATHCLYDE

DALRIADA

NORTHUMBRIA

Catterick

WALES

MERCIA

WHAT HAPPENED NEXT?

The city of Rome was sacked by the Goths in AD 410 and sacked from the sea by Vandals in AD 455. It ceased to be a Roman city in AD 476, when a German chief made himself emperor. The Roman empire as we know it had collapsed, though Roman emperors continued to reign in Constantinople until 1453.

Big changes were happening elsewhere. Some of the Scots from Ireland settled in western Scotland, where they became so powerful that they began fighting the Picts.

Southern Scotland was divided into two Celtic kingdoms, Strathclyde and Gododdin; the peoples of both kingdoms were known as Britons. Meanwhile much of the rest of Britain had been occupied by invading Angles, Saxons, and Jutes from northern Europe.

The chief place in Gododdin was Din Eidyn, the fort of Eidyn (now Edinburgh). As the Angles swept up the east coast of Britain and set up their own kingdom of Northumbria, Gododdin became sandwiched between the Angles to the south and the Picts to the north. Around AD 600, the king of

Gododdin got together a small army of between 300 and 360 fighting men, including a party of knights from Wales, and rode out against the Angles' capital at Catterick in Yorkshire. They had a long way to go. When they got there they fought like demons, but it was no good. Only four men returned from that campaign. The Angles took Din Eidyn and the lands of Gododdin, and settled there themselves.

There were four peoples now in Scotland: the Scots, the Picts, the Britons, and the Angles. In about AD 800 they were joined by a fifth, the Norsemen (or Vikings), who came first as raiders and then as settlers.

The Romans had tried to occupy the whole of Scotland, but never succeeded, in spite of four separate invasions. In time the Scots took over the lands of the Picts and the kingdom of Strathclyde,

One of the four men who returned from the attack on Catterick was a Welshman called Aneirin. He wrote a poem about the ill-fated expedition.

defeated the Angles, and regained almost all the territory occupied by the Vikings. All these ancient peoples, the Scots, the Picts, the Britons, the Angles, and the Vikings, contributed to the making of modern Scotland.

The original Gaelic language of Scotland was brought by the Celts from Ireland. The language known as Scots developed from the English spoken by the Angles who first settled in south-east Scotland. Later arrivals brought with them words and ways of speech taken from the Vikings who had settled in the parts of England from which they came.

The Romans left nothing directly, but life in Scotland today would be very different without the Roman inventions which have come to us in other ways.

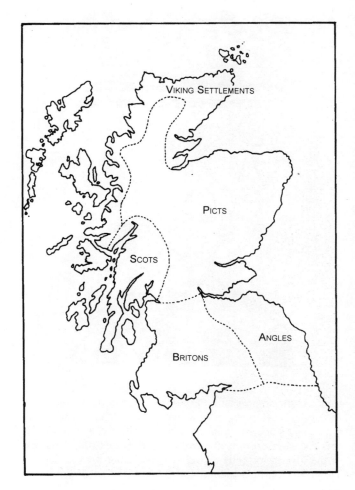

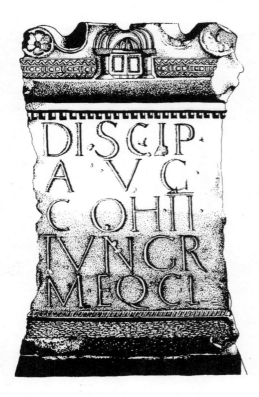

Roman lettering on an altar-stone dedicated to the goddess *Discipulina Augusta,* whose worship was encouraged by the army, since *discipulina* means 'military discipline'. It was found in the fort at Birrens in Dumfriesshire. The rest of the inscription tells us that it was erected by the Second Tungrian Cohort, which included a troop of cavalry.

OUR ROMAN HERITAGE

Our alphabet is exactly the same as the Roman alphabet, except that the Romans had no J, U, or W, which were added later. (In Latin the letter I was written for the sounds 'i' and 'j', and V for 'u', 'v', and 'w'.) Latin remained the language of scholarship until the seventeenth century and is the language of the Roman Catholic Church. About one-third of the words we use are based on Latin, and many Latin phrases survive in English today.

The calendar which Julius Caesar introduced in 46 BC, with seven months of 31 days, four of 30 days, and one of 28 days (29 days every fourth year), has, with one slight adjustment in 1582, been used ever since.

Scots law, unlike English law, is closely based on the system invented by the Romans, which came to Scotland from France and Italy.

The Romans had banks, public education and hospitals, social benefits, a daily newspaper, a postal system, a fire service, and a public water system. They built blocks of flats, and houses with central heating, running water, glass windows, and drainage.

INDEX

Some Places to Visit

- *Antonine Wall* – See map page 45.
- *Hadrian's Wall* – Housesteads Roman Fort and Museum; Vindolanda Museum; Roman Army Museum at Carvoran.
- *Dumfries Museum* (Roman exhibits and carved stones).
- *Callendar House,* Falkirk (Roman exhibits).
- *Hunterian Museum,* Glasgow University (Roman and Celtic exhibits).
- *Huntly House Museum,* Edinburgh (Roman exhibits).
- *Kilmartin House,* Kilmartin, Argyll (Celtic displays and reconstructions). Also surrounding area.
- *Museum of Scotland,* Chambers Street, Edinburgh: 'Early People' Gallery (Celtic and Roman displays). Opening 30 November 1998.
- *Scottish Crannog Centre,* Kenmore, Loch Tay (reconstruction and displays). April through October.
- *Trimontium Exhibition,* Melrose (Roman and Celtic displays).
- *Whithorn Priory and Museum,* Wigtown (Candida Casa).
- Remains of brochs include Mousa, Shetland; Gurness, Orkney; Glenelg, Lochalsh; Edinshall, Cockburn Law, Duns.
- Remains of earth-houses include Culsh, Kincardineshire; Ardestie and Carlungie, Angus; Pitcur, Perthshire.
- Other Celtic sites include Traprain Law fort, East Lothian; Castle Law fort and earth-house, East Lothian; Caterthuns forts, Angus; Dumyat ('Fort of the Maeatae'), Bridge of Allan; Burnswark fort, Ecclefechan.
- Pictish carvings are included in displays at Anthropological Museum, Marischal College, Aberdeen; McManus Galleries, Dundee; Dunrobin Castle Museum, Sutherland; Elgin Museum; Glasgow Art Galleries and Museum; Groam House Museum, Rosemarkie; Inverness Museum; Meigle Museum; St Andrews Cathedral Museum; St Vigean's Museum, Arbroath.

For information about whom to contact for further details of these and other places to visit, ring Scottish Tourist Board 0131 332 2433.